7 Legacy Steps

to

Building

Generational Wealth

by Kaye A. Williams

Foreword by Dr. Alisha "Ali" Griffith

This book is designed to provide accurate information with respect to the subject matter covered. It is sold with the understanding that the publisher is not engaged in rendering legal, financial, accounting, tax or other professional advice. This text is not a substitute for personalized advice from a knowledgeable professional. If expert assistance is required, consult the services of a competent licensed professional.

7 Legacy Steps to Building
Generational Wealth

ISBN: 9798479944499

Dedication

To God, who gives me strength;

To my Mother Grace Glentricia Foster, "Amazing Grace", whose sensible and highly effective money management skills few could ever match; and whose legacy of love, value systems and commitment to excellence provided me with a rich inheritance;

To my family: my husband Ronald, our children Jonathan, Makayla and Lianna, who give me daily inspiration.

Acknowledgements

This book is the result of years of conversations with my husband Ronald Williams and my father Keith Foster, about business, economics, finance, and life in general.

Thanks to God for nudging me. He made me aware that the series of thoughts floating in my head had to be brought to life.

To Lorraine Edwards, for project management, cover art and unwavering support.

And thanks to my clients for honouring me with your perspectives, experiences and insights.

About the author

Kaye A. Williams, BA., LL.B, MCIArb is an Attorney-at-Law whose practice is in commercial law, Property and Estates. She was awarded a UK Commonwealth Fellowship, Law and Governance from the Law Society of England and Wales.

Kaye is passionate about helping entrepreneurs and professionals adopt personal planning as part of a success mindset. In this book she provides simple, practical steps that anyone can take to start the generational wealth-building journey today.

She may be contacted at:

7LegacySteps@gmail.com

Reviews

"I don't do what I do just for myself. My greatest fulfillment comes from helping entrepreneurs exceed their limits. Like a mother who is so proud of her daughter, my heart is so filled with joy at the accomplishments of Kaye Williams – Mother, Attorney, Entrepreneur and now an Amazon best-selling author of *'7 Legacy Steps to Building Generational Wealth'*. Thank you for trusting me."

-Susie Carder
CEO, SC Consulting #1 Best Selling Author

"The author, Kaye A. Williams, thoroughly defines the steps to wealth for present and future generations. She delves into why financial planning and mentoring are the keys to building and passing on generational wealth.

Rarely are we taught these lessons, yet they are imperative to stop living from paycheck to paycheck.

Ms. Williams shares in-depth advice, including examples and actionable steps, for guided implementation. The book is educational, eye-opening, and an essential read for all."

-Jessima Murray
Ontario, Canada
Author: *Son of Barbados: A Canadian Journey, Biography of Eric Murray*

"I really enjoyed reading '7 Legacy Steps to Building Generational Wealth'! ...The book is engaging, gives spiritual and practical principles and I love the real life stories and assessments!

It is a book I will buy and implement in my household."

-Dr. Wanda M. Coleman
Ohio, USA
Founder, *Wanda M. Coleman Ministries*
Speaker, Best-selling Author, Radio Show Host

"Every chapter is full of golden nuggets designed to enrich your soul, your family and ultimately your pocket for generations to come"

-Jacqueline P. Devonish
London, England

"I am amazed and in awe of the content included in this book. The background information, the biblical references and examples from today's society.

This book does a great job tying it all together. I'm inspired by what others have done and am looking forward to creating my own legacy for my children and my children's children. It's helpful to have a reminder to think beyond today and my own aspirations in order to create something bigger and longer lasting.

Thank you Kaye for your knowledge, wisdom and encouragement to dream and plan big!

-Leslie Williams, MS-HCA
California, USA

Transformational Coach

"Kaye Williams asks the one question that few can answer. "How will my family sustain financial stability after I'm gone?" In her easy to read, yet straight forward approach, Kaye asks the questions and gives straight forward answers to building generational wealth. Her 7-step blueprint will show you how to build your financial legacy starting right where you are."

-Saundra Gilliard
Founder and CEO of *Femininely Free!* focused on helping women live authentically.
www.https://femininelyfree.com

Table of Contents

Foreword

It has been a pleasure to support, strategize and co-create with Kaye Williams. As a business strategist and coach, speaking to hundreds of thousands of women, about the importance of legacy launching, this literary piece was refreshing and I felt reinvigorated to read more about simple steps and tools to build generational wealth and legacy, immediately.

As the author states, legacy is not only about money, but it's "about the impact you are making on your family, friends and the world, today and in the future."

My favorite parts in this book include specific suggestions on how to get clear on your goals. I also loved the tools given on creating the plan and managing the wealth during the building process.

With over 25 years of practice as an Attorney-at-Law, Kaye has been equipped and is experienced in working with clients in business, estate planning and has researched the success in legacy building for multi-generational wealth.

As a Mom and Entrepreneur, Kaye is passionate about the importance of creating and teaching our future generations the value of living with a success mindset, creating ongoing legacy planning, normalizing conversations in wealth building and organizing personal, estate and business affairs, over time.

I coach busy professional Moms to launch their own brands online, so that they can create legacy-driven businesses. This book provides the tools on activating generational wealth planning, strategies on the execution of ongoing legacy building and the steps on how to make it happen.

-Dr. Alisha "Ali" Griffith,
Biz Strategist and Coach,
Best Selling Author
and Global Speaker

www.draligriffith.com

Introduction

This book is dedicated to those who we would define as 'Legacy Makers' or 'Legacy Builders': first- and second-generation entrepreneurs or professionals and those with an entrepreneurial mindset.

You are the generation making those 'power moves' within your lifetime to build, and to create. You care deeply about doing good in the world. It's not merely about building wealth, but also about preserving it to make things better for future generations.

Valuable lessons have been learnt along your journey and you want to pass on those golden nuggets of truth. You have given a lot and yet have so much more to give. It has become important to you that those whom you love can enjoy what you've built and more importantly, the next generation can set out on their own journey to expand upon what you have created.

Growing up, my parents made me read: fiction, non-fiction, literature of every kind.

Back then with no internet, no cable, and international news broadcasts in a one-hour slot once per day, my window to the big wide world arrived by local delivery once per week: *Time, Newsweek, The Economist,* and British broad sheet newspapers. Once a month, there was *Reader's Digest.*

And so began my journey of voraciously reading news and current affairs, lifestyle and entertainment, business and economics. Apart from other interests, I was always curious about the stories, fortunes and misfortunes of the wealthy, a favourite topic across the weekly literature.

We lived on an island which was one of their known playgrounds, and unofficial, whispered stories would abound. It was viewed for the most part as 'dynastic behavior' to borrow a phrase used by Warren Buffett, CEO of Berkshire Hathaway CEO. Warren Buffet is of the view that such behavior will likely lose its appeal one day[1]. For me, it sparked a deeper questioning about inherited wealth.

Over 25 years of practice as an Attorney-at-Law, and as an observer of society generally, I was concerned by what seemed to be a pattern whereby a successful first- or second-generation businesses, or professional practices, would suffer decline and be liquidated after its founder retired or died. There often was no succession plan.

In most cases they built such respected legacies, and were honoured in their lifetime for their achievements, but the story ended there. Maybe that was the intent. Nevertheless, I wondered about the challenges to the building and preservation of multi-generational legacies and wealth.

Within the practice of the law profession I have been honoured to

---

[1] Buffett, Warren : "Comments by Warren E. Buffett in Conjunction With His Annual Contribution of Berkshire Hathaway Shares to Five Foundations " : https://www.busineswire.com/news/home/20210623005262/en/

work with clients in business matters and estate planning. We have also had to work through areas covered by this book.

From my experiences and from my research, the success of a legacy of multi-generational wealth includes financial management, money management and creating estate plans. It also includes another layer: it lies in preparing the next generation. It's about normalizing conversations in three main areas of self-care: ongoing personal education about finances and wealth, a commitment to the family's values, culture and goals, and keeping personal affairs well organized.

It's never too early to start, it's never too late to start. Just get started.

I hope these 7 practical steps help you on your legacy journey.

CHAPTER 1:
The 'Three Generation' Rule

'For riches don't last forever, and the crown might not be passed to the next generation'

Proverbs 27:24

A study conducted globally of the world's Ultra High Net Worth (UHNW) population , that is, individuals whose net worth is 30 million or higher, revealed that the majority, 88% are 'self-made' meaning they earned their wealth in their own lifetime[2]. This is a remarkable statistic.

---

[2] Wealth-X "World Ultra Wealth Report 2021" http://go.wealthx.com/world-ultra-wealth-report-2021

The question is asked, 'what happens to those who inherited wealth?'

In Canada, it was reported from a survey[3] that only 20 per cent of millionaires attributed part of their wealth to an inheritance. 67% of Canadians with a net worth of more than $1 million made their wealth on their own.

Of that figure, one-third were women and almost half, 48%, were either immigrants or first generation Canadians.

Another study of 233 millionaires with an average wealth of 4.3 million, and who had different paths to wealth, confirmed similar findings: three-quarters or 76% were 'self-made' and a quarter - 24% - inherited wealth.

These observations are further borne out in another study. Ramsey

---

[3] Online survey was conducted by Pollara, reported in https://globalnews.ca/news/638461/two-thirds-of-affluent-canadians-are-self-made-millionaires-study/ : "Two-thirds of affluent Canadians are self-made millionaires: study"

Solutions conducted one of the largest surveys of millionaires in the United States with 10,000 participants. The survey found that 79% of millionaires did not receive any form of inheritance at all from their parents or other family members.

Why is this discussion important for Legacy builders? You have worked so hard to build, but you have wondered, how long will this legacy survive? Today the challenge is to focus as much energy on building legacy, as you do on preserving wealth.

There is an axiom called the "Three-Generation Rule Path" which has been historically observed across different cultures.

While the sayings are based on traditional wisdom studies have confirmed that 70% of wealthy families lose their wealth by the second generation, and 90% by the third generation[4].

---

[4] Study by Williams Group Wealth consultancy reported in : https://money.com/rich-families-lose-wealth/

Commonly known as 'shirtsleeves to shirtsleeves in 3 generations' it is a cycle that sees the first generation, determined to make something better for themselves, overcome hardship and achieve their goals. In their later years, their efforts have paid off and they are able to enjoy a comfortable lifestyle.

Their children, the second generation, witnessed their parent or parents struggle firsthand. While they enjoy a comfortable lifestyle, they have not forgotten the hardships and that informs their financial and educational choices.

Some preserve what they have been given and build even greater wealth. Others are unsure how to handle and grow wealth.

The third generation often do not have an entrepreneurial mindset neither do they have any concept of hardship or struggle. The values and attitudes needed to continue to build and grow wealth have not been passed on. Very often their parents are far too busy and they have not been skilled or equipped to manage the inheritance. The wealth is dissipated.

There is another factor at play. There is the issue of decline of the original business and the need to keep finding ways to build new wealth.

By the third generation, the original family business, or the market for that business may have waned. Without a clear plan for ongoing re-invention, diversification or expansion into new markets and industries, the original business may not create the same level of wealth to support a growing family.

In a study conducted in the United Kingdom of family businesses[5] only a

---

[5] "Research on Family Businesses" Paul Braidford, Maxine Houston, Gordon Allinson and Professor Ian Stone: Policy Research Group, Durham Business School/St Chad's College for the Department for Business, Innovation and Skills.
https://assets.publishing.service.gov.uk/government/
/system/uploads/attachment_data/file/3
13957/bis-14-699-research-into-family-businesses-bis-research-paper-172
uploads.pdf

minority had a clear roadmap for the succession planning and the future. This observation was largely unconnected to the size of the business.

The study noted further that reasonably consistent findings reveal only about one-third of family businesses successfully make the transition from first generation (i.e. the founder(s)) to second, and only a third subsequently make the transition to the third generation.

Merrill Private Wealth Management conducted a study of 650 American families with a minimum of 3 million in invested assets[6]. Two-thirds said they have not talked to their children about their wealth and ten percent flatly stated they never will.

Other reports have indicated [7] that 78% of first generation entrepreneurs

---

[6] "How do families make effective wealth decisions: Defining the purpose, process and perspective of family wealth " https://www.pbig.ml.com/articles/how-do-families-make-effective-wealth-decisions.html

[7] https://money.com/rich-families-lose-

are of the view that the next generation is not financially responsible enough to handle inheritance, while 64% admit they have disclosed little to nothing about their wealth to their children.

Conversely, studies have shown that multi-generational families across the world have successfully sustained wealth past the third generation[8].

The key success factors have been carefully examined.

A business plan or succession plan for family wealth is an objective document, but any discussion of multi-generational wealth has to be more nuanced, appreciating the fact that there is a living, breathing, emotional dynamic that must be taken into account[9].

When it comes to legacy and generational wealth, the best business

---

wealth/
[8] "Family Wealth Paths: A New Look at Family Wealth" Professor John Davis: https://johndavis.com/family-wealth-paths/
[9] Research in Family Businesses, p. 63

or succession plan in the world is not effective unless emotional intelligence is given primary consideration in that plan.

Traditional sayings on Multi-generational Wealth

There are many traditional sayings across the world that observe certain types of cycles of family wealth:

- ❖ *"There's nob'but three generations a'tween a clog and clog." English proverb*

- ❖ *"The third generation ruins the house." Japanese proverb*

- ❖ *"Rice paddies to rice paddies in three generations." Japanese proverb*

- ❖ *"The father buys, the son builds, the grandchild sells, and his son begs." Scottish proverb*

- ❖ *"Wealth does not last past three generations." Chinese proverb*

- ❖ *"From stalls to stars to stalls."* *Italian traditional saying*

- ❖ *"Shirtsleeves to shirtsleeves in three generations."* *American proverb*

- ❖ *"First generation, trader; second generation, gentleman; third generation, beggar."* *Spanish proverb*

These traditional proverbs and sayings have the same message: unless a clear plan is put in place, generational wealth seems to have a pattern of degeneration.

CHAPTER 2:
Building a Legacy Today: Shifts in Wealth Dynamics

There is an interesting dynamic occurring. The COVID-19 pandemic in 2020 and 2021 caused the widespread closure of businesses, and in some cases, the evaporation of certain industries, yet across the world the richest two-thirds of the world's billionaire class amassed a further 20% increase in fortunes[10].

On the other end of the scale, many have felt that the cost of living is increasing, and that 'adulting' as millennials call it, can be pricey. It seems as if the cookie cutter advice of building wealth isn't as easily attainable. We refer to that traditional advice of finish your education, get a job and move up the ranks, buy a home and invest your savings and you

---

[10] 'In 2020 the ultra-rich got richer. Now they're bracing for the backlash' Brenna Hughes Neghaiwi, Simon Jessop https://www.reuters.com/article/us-wealth-billionaires-outlook-insight-idUSKBN2BH0J7

will have built up enough wealth to retire comfortably.

There were changes in the job market even before the COVID-19 pandemic. Many changes were driven by the digital economy[11]. A 'job for life' is a thing of the past and 'contract' or fixed term employment is the norm. As a society we encountered:

- ❖ Creation of new industries and transformation of existing jobs and skills;
- ❖ Loss of jobs as certain skills were overtaken by technology. In some cases, technology practically replaced certain industries, such as travel agencies;
- ❖ Outsourcing of skills and jobs.

Long term investments such as home ownership has customarily been identified as a key component in

---

[11] OECD/Inter-American Development Bank (2016), "Skills and jobs in the digital economy", in Broadband Policies for Latin America and the Caribbean: A Digital Economy Toolkit, OECD Publishing, Paris. DOI:https://doi.org/10.1787/9789264251823-12-en

building generational wealth. That traditional advice worked well for the post war or "baby boomers' generation.

Today, however, high housing costs, student loans, the cost of food, clothing, travel – it all seems so tough to build assets traditionally. Financial reporting refers to the trend of 'BOMAD' – 'Bank Of Mum And Dad' – being responsible for funding the younger Generation X with up to 20% or one on four property transactions[12].

What do these wealth accumulation trends mean? Future generations will have to work robustly in the digital economy to accumulate savings and incomes, while carefully navigating a higher debt ratio that comes with a higher cost of living[13].

---

[12] Financial Times:

[13] Deloitte Center for Financial Services 'The future of wealth in the United States: Mapping trends in generational wealth the path to 2030' Val Srinivas and Urval Goradia
https://www2.deloitte.com/content/dam/insights/us/articles/us-generational-wealth-trends/DUP_1371_Future-wealth-in-America_MASTER.pdf

Wealth Accumulation Trends to Consider

Income gaps can be found around the world. In the United Kingdom, a report for financial year ending 2020, the income of the richest 20% of people was over six times higher than the poorest 20%, while the richest 10% received 50% more income than the poorest 40%[14].

According to a study commissioned in the USA by the National Endowment for Financial Education (NEFE)[15], 96% of adults face four or more "income shocks" during their lifetimes, which can reduce their

---

[14] Office of National Statistics: Household income inequality, UK: financial year ending 2020 (provisional) https://www.ons.gov.uk/peoplepopulatio nandcommunity/personalandhouseholdfi nances/incomeandwealth/bulletins/house holdincomeinequalityfinancial/financialy earending2020provisional

[15] New School report "Untangling the Determinants of Retirement Savings Balances: https://www.nefe.org/news/2017/08/co mmon-income-shocks-disrupt-retirement-savings.aspx

retirement savings or income by at least 10% on each occasion. Income shocks are events such as a health crisis, job loss or life transitions during the working years.

Reports of Federal Reserve data for the decade 2020 shows that there has been a shift in how wealth is created and maintained between generations. In the United States, they compared three categories of the workforce, 'Baby boomers', 'Generation X' and 'Millennials'. Baby Boomers born between 1946 and 1964, ages 56 to 74 in 2020, Generation X born between 1965 and 1980 and ages 40-55 in 2020, and millennials born 1981 and 1996 and who were ages 24 to 39 in 2020.

The data reveals that baby boomers in the USA who have accumulated wealth during their lifetime are ten 10 times wealthier than millennials and twice more wealthy than Generation X workers. At the time of reporting, baby boomers held 53.2% of US wealth or $59.96 trillion, Generation X held half of that figure, $28.5 trillion and millennials held 4.6% or $5.19 trillion.

There is trend that shows that millennials now earn 20% less than boomers did at the same age, and when average net worth was compared, there is a gap of $600,000.00 when the boomers were at the millennial's age[16].

In the United Kingdom, a study is reported by the Financial Times to state that 1 in 5 Baby boomers have a net value of a million or more[17].The primary source of their wealth was not cash, but homeownership, which, depending on location and due to market forces, increased their household wealth by an incredible 96%. The other sources of wealth for such households were pension schemes, inheritance and share portfolios.

---

[16]
https://www.businessinsider.com/millennials-versus-boomers-wealth-gap-2020-10 : "Millennials dominate the US workforce, but they're still 10 times poorer than boomers"
[17] Office for National Statistics Wealth and Assets Survey reported in the Financial Times: "One in five UK baby boomers are millionaires" by Nikou Asgari https://www.ft.com/content/c69b49de-1368-11e9-a581-4ff78404524e

CHAPTER 3:
Creating the Legacy You Want: Identify Your "Why"

'Choose life, that it may be well with you- you and your children'

Deuteronomy 30:19

LEGACY STEP 1:

Identify why you are on this Legacy Journey

Traditionally, legacy was viewed as something you leave behind when you are gone. But that mindset has shifted from focusing only on what is left behind. Legacy is today, it's right now. Legacy is about life and living. It's about learning from the past, living in the present, and building for the future.

You deserve to create the legacy you want. What is legacy? In everyday terms, legacy is about the impact you are making on your family, friends and the world, today and in the future. It isn't only about money. It could be your family, career, wealth, societal impact, community building or giving back in the way you define it.

Why should you think about your legacy journey? It enriches you. Research shows that a sense of working to create a legacy gives adults deeper meaning in their life. It also sharpens your approach to leadership.

Differing views on multi-generational wealth

Different wealth creators have their views on this topic of multi-generational wealth.

Billionaire and Berkshire Hathaway CEO Warren Buffet announced that, within his lifetime, he will give away 99% of his personal wealth to five charitable foundations. His family will likely inherit 1% of his wealth.

In a letter to shareholders he said: "Dynastic behavior is less the norm here than in most countries and its appeal will likely diminish. After much observation of super-wealthy families, here's my recommendation: Leave the children enough so that they can do anything but not enough that they can do nothing[18]"

In contrast, banking magnate Sir Nathan Rothschild had a different view. He ensured the requisite tax, estate, and investment planning was in place, but he also intentionally prepared his children (and future generations) to be independent, self-confident members of society, apart from their family wealth.

---

[18] Buffett, Warren : Comments by Warren E. Buffett in Conjunction With His Annual Contribution of Berkshire Hathaway Shares to Five Foundations https://www.businesswire.com/news/home/20210623005262/en/

He created robust organizational and decision-making processes in the family that included family communication and a solid set of shared values.

A number of tools were set up, including a family bank to encourage entrepreneurial activities, mentoring of the next generation, annual family reunions where shared values were taught, explicit expectations for family participation in group activities, and active charitable engagement within the community.

The family continues to thrive to this day *(Zeeb and Zeeb 2009).*

Be clear on your goals

Legacy Makers are often cycle breakers. Some may have the benefit of a family line of entrepreneurs and professionals.

On the other hand, just as many have said they did not have the benefit of such patterns in their family, but in their desire to break from cycles of hardship they modelled themselves after a business owner or mentor who did have that mindset.

Breaking negative generational cycles is no small achievement.

We are all subject to various and complex cycles of life and there are deep psychological processes around this topic, which is not the subject of this text. The subject is raised however, in order for you to understand this point: Sometimes you are so focused on what you *do not* want, and the cycles that you are determined to break, that you have not clearly articulated what you *do* want, and your vision for the future.

We are interested in building for the future, and specifically multi-generational wealth.

Be clear on:

- ❖ What's my highest priority in my lifetime?
- ❖ Why do I do what I do?
- ❖ Who, or what, motivates me?
- ❖ Are my life choices aligned with what motivates me?
- ❖ What gives me joy?

We will examine this in more detail in our discussion on family values. Businessman and author Jim Rohn said it this way: "We are stewards of this world, and we have a calling in our lives to leave it better than how we found it."

CHAPTER 4:
Legacy Mindset: Planning for Your Multi-Generational Future

LEGACY STEP 2:
Make a Mindset Shift: Think Generationally

There is a proverb that says "A good person leaves an inheritance to their children's children". (Proverbs 13:22) That's an inheritance for at least three generations. As we said earlier, an inheritance doesn't have to be money, it can be non-monetary, such as values, or our philosophy on life, but we will discuss this further in this book.

Even the most successful people find it challenging to map out their personal life well into the future. It is an interesting dynamic.

Entrepreneurs and professionals with an entrepreneurial mindset, by definition, can see prospective opportunities and turn them into successful outcomes. They believe in their ability to overcome challenges and take ownership of their future.

So why is it so hard to plan and organize our personal lives? We often think in general terms, 'I know what I want to be doing, or not doing, in 20 years', but to actually set out that plan in detail is a challenge.

If you have found it tough to set out your 10-year, 15-year, or 20-year personal plan, it's certainly not a flaw in your thinking.

While we are built with the capacity to think in the future, we are nevertheless wired to think in the 'now'.

Research has shown that, although the human brain is uniquely enabled to think into the vast future, the majority of us naturally skip over future long term planning and prefer to plan in small, immediate units.[19]

We naturally prefer planning the next train route or an immediate reward like getting a coffee or arranging lunch with friends We are even happy planning our next vacation.

It a process called "delay discounting[20]", which means that we naturally prefer

---

19

https://www.templeton.org/discoveries/future-mindedness : John Templeton Foundation 'Great Expectations: New insights into how and why we think about the future'

[20] Delayed reward discounting (DRD) refers to a person's preferences for smaller immediate rewards versus larger delayed rewards (i.e., how much a reward is discounted by virtue of its delay in time) (Bickel and Marsch, 2001, Madden and Bickel, 2009).

a smaller, immediate reward over a much larger but delayed reward.

It's a process that is employed in goal-setting, in particular, when a larger strategic goal is broken into immediate, short term steps. Each step is a milestone towards that larger 'delayed' reward.

Why should we plan further in the future? It is because, as Legacy Builders, business owners and entrepreneurs, there is a huge gap between the typical planning timeframes for products and services, and the planning timeframes for multi-generational wealth building.

Business planning timeframes are dictated by markets and forecasting.

The average business cycle is 4.7 years. Multi-generational planning requires a different approach.

A business owner or professional could potentially see money opportunities decades into the future, but struggle to convert that kind of vision and energy into planning for their personal lives.

The following table and chart provide the comparison:

Thinking generationally

	Average Business Plan Time frames		Average span of a generation based on scientific models
Short term	6 months – 2 years	1st Generation	25-33 years
Medium term	3-5 years	2nd Generation	50-66 years
Long term	5-10 years	3rd Generation	75-99 years

On a bar chart, the contrast would look like this:

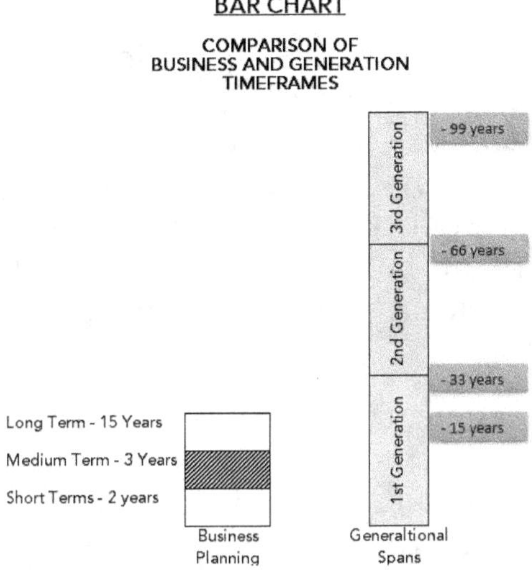

As entrepreneurs and professionals therefore, your business and career is expected to go through several cycles as your family grows. This requires a shift in thinking.

Research conducted in the UK on family business[21] stated that the companies identified the following as priorities: the creation of a sustainable long term income stream; the growth and preservation of family

---

[21] 'Research in Family Businesses'

financial and emotional wealth; and the creation of opportunities for the next generation.

Interestingly, the creation of opportunities for that next generation was seen as more important than passing on the existing business as a physical entity. However, only a minority of businesses in the study had a clear roadmap for succession planning.

The inference can be made that, as successful first-generation business owners, while your business may continue to flourish with the second or even third generation, the family business may adapt and take a different form that which exists today.

The cycle of business and professional income versus multi-generational income was also seen in another study[22] which showed that successful multi-generational businesses will see patterns of decline in some areas, however they must

---

[22] "Family Wealth Paths: A New Look at Family Wealth" Professor John Davis

maintain a willingness to look for new opportunities.

Business owners or professionals must be prepared to diversify and regenerate in order to maintain long-term success.

This is why Legacy Makers are challenged to make a mindset shift: have the two sets of thinking – business time frames and generational spans- running parallel to each other.

It appears that the critical elements to multi-generational wealth lies in two factors: first, the ability of the current generation to engage in, and implement, succession planning and second, equipping the next generation with the skills and tools necessary to take successful advantage of tomorrow's business and investment opportunities.

Questions we could ask are:

- ❖ Where would I like my business to be in 20 years? What would that look like?
- ❖ How long do I want to stay active in the business?

- ❖ What succession plan do I have in place?
- ❖ In the next 20 to 30 years, do I plan to build and expand or liquidate and divest?
- ❖ What legacy would I wish to pass on – what business and life experiences, lessons learned, family journeys (good and bad) do I want the family to remember?

Assessment Sheet:

Am I thinking Generationally?

Starting the process requires you to have an idea of where you are now. Should you wish to take a brief assessment to determine whether you are thinking generationally, you may access it here: https://www.7legacysteps.com

Studies show[23] that when you are willing to create a plan for your

---

[23] https://www.success-stream.co.uk/11-benefits-personal-development-and-plan 'Benefits of Personal Development and Creating a Plan' Rosser, Jo

future, you improve personal goal setting and achievement, decrease stress levels, improve quality of life, increase self-confidence and enrich family life.

Your family may explore their own journey before joining the family business.

In the 1980's Patricia Williams, inspired by other family members who also owned McDonald's franchises, quit her job, took a small business loan and became a McDonald's Owner/Operator in a prime location in Los Angeles.

In the 1990's she saw an opportunity. She traded her one prime location for five restaurants in what some considered less desirable neighborhoods.

Her vision was to serve those communities. The five locations became top sellers, hiring people from the area and giving back to the community.

Running an owner operated franchise while raising two daughters was tough. Her elder daughter, Nicole Enearu, gained a Bachelor's Degree in Psychology and a Master's Degree in Educational Psychology.

She spent 10 years working in the field of Social Services. She decided on a career change and bought her first store.

Nicole later went on to became the first female African American Chair for the McDonald's Southern California Regional Leadership Council. She has been honored as a next-generation Owner/Operator.

Patricia's younger daughter Kerri Harper-Howie, an Attorney, attended the University of California, Berkeley where she double majored in Political Science and Rhetoric, then to the NYU School of Law. She had a 13-year career in employment law until she also made a career shift to join the family business by purchasing her first three restaurants.

In 2017 they opened their 13th

location. Today, they operate over 18 restaurants in the LA Metro area, employing more than 700 people in the community and generating annual revenues of $50 million.

They are ardent supporters of neighborhood enterprise and charitable programs[24].

[24] Williams/Enearu Organization: "Our Story: Williams/Enearu/Harper-Howie" https://wemcd.com/our-story and BlackBusiness.com: "This Mom and Her Two Daughters Own 13 McDonald's Franchises in California": https://www.blackbusiness.com/2017/07/black-women-mother-daughters-own-13-mcdonalds-franchises-los-angeles.html

CHAPTER 5:
The Legacy of Money Management and Financial Mentoring

Proverbs 21:5

LEGACY STEP 3:
Adopt a Lifestyle of Learning and Mentoring

Imagine you could make all the money you wanted or needed. Would that solve everything for you? But what if you or your family spend as much as you earn?   The ability to earn vast wealth is useless if lifestyle spending patterns outrun earnings.

We know that, when it comes to wealth, it's about how much money we earn as well as how we manage money. Patterns of earning and spending have to be closely examined.

Typically, families will expand, and as they do, decisions must be made with respect to the family business. Those decisions are often emotional decisions to make.

As we discussed in Chapter 1, planning involving families is not the same as setting out a business plan or mapping out a high-paying corporate career. The best laid plans based on established rules and sound advice must also have an emotional intelligence quotient.

Earlier in this book we noted[25] that a majority - 78% of first-generation entrepreneurs - are of the view that the next generation is not financially responsible enough to handle

---

25   https://money.com/rich-families-lose-wealth/

inheritance, while 64% admit they have disclosed little to nothing about their wealth to their children.

This is where financial mentoring is so important to thinking multi-generationally. We must normalize conversations about money management, responsibilities, finances and wealth.

Being intentional about ongoing education and development of financial literacy is a key component of successful legacy building and wealth transitions[26].

One other reason why mentoring is so important is that, in the traditional educational system, financial literacy is not a core subject.

Most school and college graduates are not as aware of money matters as they

---

[26] McCullough, Tom: "Preparing both 'the family' and 'the money' for the transition of wealth to the next generation" Adjunct Professor, Rotman School of Management University of Toronto https://www.rotman.utoronto.ca/Professi onalDevelopment/Executive-Programs/FeaturedArticles/Important-Lessons-for-Family-Wealth-Management

should be: the importance of maintaining a good credit score, how to secure a loan for a car, interest rates, understanding the process and responsibility of a mortgage, saving and investing wisely. They are often not fully versed on business finance terms such as return on investment, bonds, stocks, venture capital, asset management, degrees of risk. As business owners, we often had to learn difficult lessons the hard way.

In an effort to protect their family members from tough lessons, it has been observed that the older generation would shield the younger generation. But they do so at their own detriment.

Legacy Makers must also be committed to ongoing wealth creation. The initial enterprise that created the wealth for the first-generation entrepreneur or professional is the first rung of success in the ladder, but for those who wish to build multi-generational wealth they must turn to qualified asset and investment professionals to create a long-term plan for growing their portfolios.

Regardless of what career path is pursued by the second or third generation, financial mentoring is a process by which Legacy Makers take others underwing to develop the smart money skills of their mentees. Small loans can be given to encourage them to invest, save or build a business idea and report on their earnings. Loans? Yes, loans, so they practice the concept of borrowing, making a return and servicing debt.

Along with understanding finance and investment terms, this exercise must be repeated consistently. Solid money management skills must be seen as life skills.

A five-year study of millionaires found that there was a pattern of four main types of approaches to growing money: Saver-Investors, Big Company Climbers, Virtuosos, and Entrepreneurs[27]. Your mentee will

----

[27] Tom Corley CPA, author of "Rich Habits: The Daily Success Habits of Wealthy Individuals" :

likely naturally be more comfortable in one or more of these patterns. The challenge is to recognize and encourage those abilities.

Think of it: you successfully achieved your wealth because you either were mentored or you were committed to lifelong self-education. Perhaps both. The same must be encouraged in the next generation at any age or stage.

Financial mentoring can begin at an early age with young children. Practical financial mentoring can also occur during university or college, or as young adults seek car purchases or approach the goal of homeownership.

If the next generation is grown, financial mentoring can take the form of regular discussions and ongoing education through short courses. A list with suggestions on how to get started with financial mentoring is available   here: https://www.7legacysteps.com

---

https://grow.acorns.com/habits-millionaires-have-in-common/

You may be reluctant because approaching this may be awkward, difficult or may even give rise of conflict. You may think they are not interested. It takes courage. Turn to a qualified professional for help if necessary.

Most importantly however, share your stories. Financial mentoring doesn't start with the attitude "I've done this perfectly, so do as I say'. It comes from a place of authenticity: 'I made mistakes, learnt my lessons, and here's what worked'.

It's also about the first generation sharing fundamental principles but recognizing that markets and industries change. What worked for you may not work for the next generation.

Remember, it's a mindset shift, an intentional step towards normalizing conversations around legacy, responsibility, money and multi-generational wealth. It's never too early, it's never too late. And there's never a perfect time to start, so just start.

CHAPTER 6:
Acknowledge the Journey, Establish New Traditions

Deuteronomy 6:7

LEGACY STEP 4:
Create Your Family Vision

Brian Lara, legendary international cricketer now businessman and philanthropist, was quoted as saying: "You just don't pick up family values, unless your parents teach you and let you know exactly what they expect."

One of the common success factors among families who effectively maintained multi-generational wealth is staying focused on family values. In referring to family, we refer to your biological family, or the unit, or the community you have chosen to be your family.

Some first-generation Legacy Makers have the full support of friends and family and may have role models, mentors and the benefit of clearly articulated values to guide them on the entrepreneurial journey.

Others however must deal with negative, toxic relationships, even ridicule, when they broke away and chose the entrepreneurial journey. Other family members may be neutral, but not supportive. Some are bewildered by your actions, but love and support you anyway.

Right now in your legacy journey you should be aware of your values and the wonderful vision you have for yourself and your family. So discuss and communicate them. It is much easier to know what you don't want. It's much harder to figure out what you do want.

When developing family values, it may help to think about where the family has come from, where it wants to go, and the plan to get there:

- ❖ Past: Acknowledge all aspects of the family history, including the great, the 'not-so-great' and everything in between.

- ❖ Present: Confirm and honour the values that have served you well, the ones that have made you a success today.

- ❖ Future: Set out clear values for the future – you may not see them manifested yet, but you are committed to working towards them.

Not everyone can be brought in on this exercise with you. Surrounding yourself with positive supportive people has to be the priority.

Decide who will be included in the journey.

Building Legacy: Family Values Assessment © :

A goal or a plan always begins with an assessment of where you are, so you can decide where you want to be.

Try the following assessment, with the number 1 for 'No, it doesn't exist' and number 10 for 'Absolutely, this is well established'. There is no perfect score nor perfect answer. The point of the assessment is to inspire you to think about aspects of your legacy journey:

I have, or my family has, the following:	▢
. A Family motto or mission statement	
. We discuss our Family motto or mission statement	
. We have religious or moral values/ guiding principles	
. We have a clear vision for the future	
We have clear values on:	
. Personal responsibility	

. Work ethic	
. Resolving conflict	
. Respecting opinions of others	
. Acknowledging, honoring and celebrating each other	
. Money	
. Leadership	
. Charitable giving	
. Volunteering time	
We discuss:	
. Family values & culture	
. Life lesson stories (good and bad)	
. Money and Business	
. How we can help others	
There are opportunities for family members to grow into leadership roles	
As a family we meet regularly (in person or virtually) to discuss:	
. Organizational affairs	
. Business or Investments	
. To celebrate	
As a family we play together regularly with:	
. Unstructured social time	
. Vacations	
. Family games	

<table>
<tr><td>. Bond over shared sports,
    interests or cultural activities</td><td></td></tr>
</table>

Celebratory meetings, dinners and events are a wonderful way to intentionally honour, support and strengthen your family's stated values. The legacy can grow in the following ways:

- ❖ storytelling
- ❖ family games
- ❖ sharing old family photos
- ❖ acknowledging all aspects of the past

Such events could be inclusive, celebrating each member that attends. The values can be brought to life on each occasion.

Author and speaker Dave Ramsey shares an example on discovering family values [28].

His family was known as a 'hardworking bunch', with varying

---

[28] Ramsey, Dave 'The Legacy Journey: A Radical View of Biblical Wealth and Generosity' 2014 Ramsey Press

degrees of financial success. He traced his ancestry and discovered his family was of Scottish descent.

On a family trip to Scotland, he toured the Ramsey Castle and, as he entered, saw a huge coat of arms with two words in Latin: *Ora et Labora*, translated "Pray and Work".

Seeing that ancient coat of arms struck him because hundreds of years later, an entire world away, his family in the USA were also known for those two things: prayer and work.

CHAPTER 7
Building The Legacy: Calculating Your Net Worth

'Be diligent and fully aware of the condition of your flock, and pay close attention to your herds.'

Proverbs 27:23

LEGACY STEP 5:
Regularly Set Clear Goals for Your Net Worth

We are challenging ourselves to make mindset shifts in our legacy journey.

It is well documented that certain steps, such as home ownership, or real estate in general, are one of surest ways to build net worth over time.

Real estate investment, like any other investment, has its risks. It requires that you actively take the time to learn the successful strategies that will yield the best results.

Whether your portfolio comprises savings, investments, or real estate, be a savvy, active investor. Seek the services of competent, licensed professionals.

Even if you have someone advising you, be aware of the tax, regulatory and legal environment for your investments.

Calculate Your Net Worth

If you haven't done so already, I would like to challenge you to regularly calculate and set positive targets as it relates to your net worth. Why? As you build wealth, you may take risks. But risk has to be balanced.

Calculating your net worth gives you a clear picture of your financial health and where you want to go in your journey.

What is net worth?

Assets – Liabilities = Your Net Worth

Your net worth can have a positive balance or a negative balance. Naturally, we want to maintain our net worth with a positive balance!

Your assets are anything of value that you own that can be converted into cash. Examples include investments, bank and brokerage accounts, retirement funds, real estate and personal property (vehicles, jewelry, art, and collectibles)—and, of course, cash itself.

Intangibles such as your "business goodwill" or a powerful influencer image are often considered assets as well.

Your liabilities, on the other hand, represent your debts, such as loans, lines of credit, mortgages, credit card debt, medical bills, and student loans.

The difference between the total value of your assets and liabilities is your net worth. Once you have identified your net worth right now, you can now set short, medium and long term goals.

Building Your Net Worth

Simple ways to build your net worth are:

- ❖ Make a plan to reduce liabilities;
- ❖ Review: make a plan to increase assets;
- ❖ Invest in homeownership or property;
- ❖ Be prepared to look at long-term savings and investments that help your money to grow;
- ❖ Explore additional revenue streams.

You may access a net worth calculation and goal setting worksheet here: https://www.7legacysteps.com

Keep debts at manageable levels to buffer 'Income Shocks'

Legacy Makers need to be aware that 'income shocks' will likely occur. At least four in the average lifetime, according to researchers[29]. Income shocks are those big life events which will affect your finances: a health crisis, leading to high medical bills; loss of income whether caused by job loss, a business deal folded, or loss of investments; divorce/separation; life transitions of one kind or another.

Sometimes, two or three income shocks occur around the same time. This is not uncommon.

Being aware of this possibility means that your plans must include buffers to counter income shocks. Buffers are such things as savings, insurance, pension and retirement plans.

Another buffer can be created by ensuring, where possible, that your assets are debt free, or the debt to

---

[29] The New School, "Untangling the Determinants of Retirement Savings Balances." Teresa Ghilarducci, Ph.D., and Anthony Webb, Ph.D. report commissioned by National Endowment for Financial Education https://www.nefe.org/news/2017/08/common-income-shocks-disrupt-retirement-savings.aspx

asset ratio is low. It is estimated that adults are saving less than a third of what is needed to retire comfortably.

If you have a million-dollar home or lifestyle, but your debts are just as high, your net worth position is fragile.

We have seen this example time and time again: a business person or entrepreneur is seemingly very successful. They have all the physical symbols of wealth: fabulous properties, cars, enviable lifestyle.

Unknown to the outside world, the assets are over-leveraged. There may also be credit card bills, loans with high rates of interest, and very little cash in hand.

As a result of an income shock, they are forced to liquidate assets, they lose on investments and properties go into foreclosure. The family suffers so much loss, grief and conflict.

Our mindset shift in this area is to shift towards building wealth. Your goals should include reducing your liabilities and determining ways in which you can increase your net worth.

Net worth fluctuates, therefore it is in your best interest to calculate every year, and set new annual to five-year targets.

The Michael Jackson Estate

Earnings have to be matched by the management of money. The fortunes of the King of Pop Michael Jackson have been widely reported for decades. His spending however far outpaced his income.

Forbes magazine stated that he was estimated to have earned over a billion dollars across the span of his solo career[30]. He earned over $500 million in performances and his own music alone and invested in a

---

[30]Forbes Magazine: https://www.forbes.com/sites/zackomalleygreenburg/2018/08/29/michael-jackson-at-60-the-king-of-pop-by-the-numbers/?sh=334d9f6e72ed

music catalogue that is today worth over 2 billion.

With lifestyle spending reported to cost $30 to $50 million per year, he exhausted his earnings, and borrowed $380 million against his catalogue. He then spent the entire loan proceeds. At the time of his death, the Estate was almost $500 million dollars in debt.

In the years following his passing the Estate embarked on an aggressive financial plan to save the assets and in particular, the music catalogue. It faced many challenges, including a battle with the IRS over the Estate value and the taxes owed.

The Estate has now paid the debts and has earned over 2 billion dollars, the highest earning celebrity estates worldwide.

CHAPTER 8:
The Legacy of Giving Back, and Paying It Forward

'The person who gives
is more blessed than
the person who
receives.'

Acts 30:25

LEGACY STEP 6:
Make Giving a Part of Your Legacy Journey

You have heard the term "pay it forward" which means that at some point in your journey someone saw your potential and invested money, time or mentorship. In turn, you respond to the kindness you receive by being kind to someone else.

'Giving back' is to return to your roots, to those institutions that helped shape you and contribute to their good work.

Whether you are going to 'give back' or 'pay it forward', giving is a central part of the legacy journey.

You may ask: 'if I am working so hard to build wealth, why should I be focused on giving?' In the context of multi-generational wealth, you are also building a lasting vision for your contribution to your community, to causes that mean the most to you.

Giving is a very uplifting experience since it frees your mind from thinking that there is not enough in the world. Giving teaches you that there is plenty to go around, and it will cause you to attract more good things in your life.

There are times when you can just send a donation. However, you challenge yourself to do more, because the focus is on building legacy.

Here are some practical ways that you can incorporate active giving into your multi-generational legacy journey:

1. **Give annually to charity or organization with a good track record.** Discuss it as a family, make sure the charity or organization stands for values which you hold dear.

   Take the time to attend their activities and see their projects. You may wish to form your own charity, foundation or non-profit.

2. **Establish a grant or annual gift in the name of a beloved family member:** Wherever you are in the legacy journey, this is a step that can be easily implemented. The grant or gift does not have to be large.

   Make sure that each year, family and friends come together to make the presentation. Get to know the recipient and encourage them in their educational or career journey.

This exercise incorporates many of the components of building and celebrating legacy: it honours family members, reinforces family values and creates opportunities for teachable moments.

3. **Volunteer your time every year:** soup kitchens, serving meals, free clinics, building homes - this should be done as a family. In building wealth, families have discovered that there is a risk of creating a sense of entitlement among the third and fourth generations.

Volunteering time is one way to build compassion and empathy. It creates gratitude, an appreciation for what you have.

4. **Give of your talent:** free clinics, mentoring – giving of your talent is a great way to

'pay it forward' to someone in need of a helping hand.

CHAPTER 9:
Organize your Affairs and keep them Organized

LEGACY STEP 7:
Organize Your Personal Affairs: It's a Success Habit!

In this Legacy step we will look at two areas:

1. organizing your personal documentation and
2. estate planning.

You can't successfully run a business without a plan. Every flight must have a flight plan and every road trip should have a road map.

You are on a Legacy journey, setting goals and plans for every area of your life. Setting out your personal affairs is no different.

Organize your personal records – and keep them organized

Have all your information - from birth certificates to retirement benefits, insurance policies to investments - organized and documented.

This is not an end of life exercise, it's a gift of life. It makes you feel informed, up to date and in control of your affairs.

So make that mindset shift and approach this exercise as a celebration of life. It is part of a success mindset.

Confidentiality

Whether you organize manually or electronically, ensure that your information is fully secured.

The key to this exercise is to have your information organized and readily accessed if necessary.

Throughout this process you should balance your right to privacy and confidentiality with your need to confide in at least one person in whom you can trust.

If regrettably you must change the person in whom you confide, make sure to make all the relevant adjustments to the place of storage, passwords etc, before informing them of your decision.

Schedule time regularly

Some of you may have this all organized already. However, if you haven't already begun this process, or you have but it's still scattered, don't be daunted.

Take it one step at a time. Schedule it routinely, and start with the records that are easiest to find.

SAMPLE CHECKLIST **I honour myself and those I love; therefore, I will organize my personal affairs as an act of self-care**		☑
My Identity	Birth, marriage, divorce, citizenship	
My children/ parents/ someone who depends on me:	Children's birth certificates, your parent's records;	
My finances:	Bank and brokerage accounts, investment information, loans, promissory or surety notes;	
My business partners and associates;	Any agreements; money due to me or money owed;	
My liabilities:	Loans (other than mortgage) credit card debts, other debts due;	
My advisors;	Names of your tax, accounting, legal, investment, broker or other advisors;	
My benefits and plans:	Retirement, pension, Government benefits; update any beneficiary information;	
My home:	All documents related to title, taxes, insurance, mortgage. If your title is kept at a bank or in a safety deposit box, make a note where it is stored. If you renovated or built the home, any key records or permissions	

	related to construction;	
Other Real Estate:	Records relating to any other properties you have bought or inherited: title, taxes, insurance, mortgages;	
Other insurance policies:	Whether term or life insurance;	
My vehicle or vehicles:	Vehicle information, valuations, loans, releases;	
Other sources of income;	Details related to these income sources	
Any leases:	Whether you are a landlord or tenant;	
My employment:	Past or present employment, length of service, employment records; awards	
My service in the military (if applicable):	Discharge information, record of service, any benefits;	
My health:	Medical benefits, medical coverage, medical records, name of your doctors and specialists;	
My pets, livestock, animals	Pet records	
My passwords, my internet presence;		

Estate Planning

Let's take a deep breath. Now exhale. Estate planning.

Over the years clients have said this is a conversation they know they should have, but one they don't want to think about.

If you can relate to that, here's where we have to make the biggest mindset shifts.

Remember in Chapter 2 we asked about your 'Why'? Who are you doing this for? This section takes you right back to asking yourself 'Why do I want to build wealth for myself, my loved ones, for my family?"

Let's approach estate planning in a similar manner as any other goal setting. We all know that successful planning is about goal setting. Coaches often say, 'begin with the end in mind'. Estate planning is not the end, it helps you to forecast for the present and future.

If you systematically think through what you want for yourself (travel, comfortable retirement) and what you want to give, and to whom, it helps you create plans today for that will be implemented in years to come. Do you understand now why estate planning helps you to be better at personal goal setting?

During your legacy journey you recognize that life is dynamic. People and circumstances ebb and flow, and they can shift. Families go through many different dynamics over the years as well. Your estate plans should also have the capacity to respond to the inevitable changes which occur.

Tough Decisions

There may be some tough decisions to think through, and that's okay. This is why you should start this process and revisit it systematically. Some have to make decisions about family members with debilitating chronic conditions, children with special needs, children battling addiction, or 'spendthrift' children. Reach out for the best advice.

Ask questions, engage in the process

For estate planning, it is recommended that you do seek professional services. That notwithstanding, the process shouldn't be left up to advisors alone.

It is recommended that you do your own research, make this an active process, and establish a plan that incorporates the legacy journey we have been discussing.

Wills & Living Trusts

When you think of estates, making a will or establishing a living trust (depending your jurisdiction) immediately comes to mind. And it should. A will is a legal document that will name beneficiaries, that is, the people you want to receive your property.

Property left by a will is subject the probate process. In some jurisdictions, particularly in the USA, the probate process can be very lengthy and costly.

This lengthy process can cost the beneficiaries. For example, if an estate is in the probate process and access to cash on bank accounts are on hold during the process, it can cause a measure of hardship to the family unless there are other cash resources.

In a situation where estate cash is on hold due to the probate process and there is a property with a mortgage, the mortgage installments must be paid otherwise the house could potentially lose value or end in foreclosure while waiting on the probate process.

Be aware of the provisions for your country. Not all jurisdictions encounter this issue of delays which can affect estate property.

In some countries a living trust has been said to be preferable. Property is set up in a trust, and it simply transfers to beneficiaries at the appropriate time. No probate or court proceeding is required.

There are also other forms of estate planning that can be set up which allows for transfers to the beneficiaries without waiting on the probate process. It doesn't require legal fees either. Examples are joint accounts, joint property, naming a beneficiary to a policy or pension plan.

Read as much as you can to understand your options in estate planning before making any decisions. However, at the end of the day, make that mindset shift and put that plan in place. There are advisors who can assist you with an estate plan to reflect your wishes.

Taxes

Estates usually have to file a final tax return with the relevant revenue authority. Apart from that, there inheritances taxes in some countries, and not in others.

Let this be an active process, and be aware of the tax provisions for your country, state or province. In most cases taxes apply to estates over a certain value. In the UK, it is Succession and Estate Duties, in the USA Estate taxes at the state and federal level. A capital gains tax may even be applicable. Some countries do not have estate inheritance tax.

There are some resources that allow you to look at estate planning for yourself, although it is best to hire a professional.

Be active in your selection, ask questions and ensure you are hiring the very best for your price bracket.

It's my birthday!

Remember, life is dynamic. You are on a legacy journey! Our personal plans should have an element of flexibility that reflects and responds to those changes. This is a part of our legacy and success mindset. We said this is part of our approach to be intentional, setting out to do these things as a celebration of life, not as an end-of-life task.

With a couple of exceptions, for example irrevocable trusts, you must be aware that you have the power to change, amend or revoke as you think necessary.

The only limitation, of course, is that you must have the mental capacity and competence to execute such changes.

You shouldn't make frequent changes to your estate plans, however, you should conduct regular reviews.

Once you have your estate plan established, and all your personal documentation organized, it is recommended that you undertake systematic reviews to confirm that your plan is in keeping with current circumstances and with what you want.

There will be occasions when you will review it, only to be satisfied to leave it exactly where it is.

You should re-look your estate plans on the occasion of either:

1. a life event or
2. a milestone birthday.

Life events:

Have you experienced any of the following recently? Here are some reasons why you should undertake an estate review:

- ❖ **Purchased or sold major assets**, such as family home, large business transactions, significant investments;

- ❖ **Married, planning to get married, or you are in a long-standing committed relationship**: be aware of the provisions in your country or state for a spouse's right to property. If you are a blended family, have discussions on what provisions you wish to make, and for whom.

- ❖ **Divorced**: this can significantly change your financial circumstances. Remember to update your beneficiary information!

- ❖ Other **major changes in financial circumstances**;

- ❖ **Birth or adoption** of a child or grandchild;

- ❖ You need to change the person you previously named in your plans;

- ❖ One of your beneficiaries passed away;

- ❖ Moved to a new state, relocated to different country, changed jobs.

Milestone birthdays

Here's another suggestion that may help with making that shift: Whenever you have an upcoming birthday that ends in zero "0" or five "5", review your estate plan and your personal organization documents we discussed.

Ask yourself; 'Do I need to change anything?' 'Should it all stay the same?'

Whatever you decide, congratulations! You have now shifted to a mindset of implementing legacy planning for yourself and your estate, not with attitude of dread, but rather as an act of self-care.

CHAPTER 10
The 7-Step Legacy Plan

Let's take the Step!

In this legacy journey we have discovered:

- ❖ 'Wealth' can and should include your values and your culture. It includes working with those whom you love to give them the very best chances for success in the future.

- ❖ Unless a clear plan is put in place, there is no guarantee that your wealth will be passed to the next generation.

Success lies in being intentional: planning, setting goals and following through on the plans.

Here is a summary of the 7 Steps:

The 7 Legacy steps towards building Multi-generational Wealth ©		☑
Legacy Step 1:	Identify why you are on this Legacy Journey	
Legacy Step 2:	Make a Mindset shift: Think Generationally	
Legacy Step 3:	Adopt a lifestyle of learning and Financial Mentoring	
Legacy Step 4:	Create your Family Vision	
Legacy Step 5:	Regularly set clear goals for your Net Worth	

Legacy Step 6:	Make Giving a part of your legacy journey	
Legacy Step 7:	Organize your personal affairs: it's a success habit	

Be happy, Stay happy!

The best things in life are indeed free: a swim on a warm day, sunrise, sunsets, a big hug from someone you love.

In my view, wealth should be directed positively: to promote well-being, to make lives better. Most importantly, even while building wealth, engage frequently in activities that bring you joy, satisfaction and make your life full of purpose.

Here's to your success in the legacy journey!

<u>**Useful resources**</u>:

The following text is a useful resource for business owners:

Carder, Susie *Power Your Profits: How to Take Your Business from $10,000 to $10,000,000* (New York: Simon & Schuster Inc.2020)

<u>**Contact Us**</u>

Have a comment or question? Would like to learn more? You may contact or visit us at:

Website:
www.7Legacysteps.com

Email:
7LegacySteps@gmail.com

Facebook:
www.facebook.com/7LegacySteps

Instagram:
www.instagram.com/7legacysteps

Twitter:
@7legacysteps

LinkedIn:
Kaye A. Williams

www.ingramcontent.com/pod-product-compliance
Lightning Source LLC
Chambersburg PA
CBHW051757250726
48659CB00001B/462